TOOLS FOR CAREGIVERS

- **ATOS:** 0.6
- **GRL:** C
- **WORD COUNT:** 25

- **CURRICULUM CONNECTIONS:** transportation

Skills to Teach

- **HIGH-FREQUENCY WORDS:** go, is, let's, one, see, the, this, us
- **CONTENT WORDS:** blue, deck, green, help, red, skateboards, wheels
- **PUNCTUATION:** apostrophe, exclamation marks, periods
- **WORD STUDY:** long /e/, spelled ee (*green*, *see*, *wheels*); /oo/, spelled ue (*blue*); multisyllable word (*skateboards*)
- **TEXT TYPE:** factual description

Before Reading Activities

- Read the title and give a simple statement of the main idea.
- Have students "walk" through the book and talk about what they see in the pictures.
- Introduce new vocabulary by having students predict the first letter and locate the word in the text.
- Discuss any unfamiliar concepts that are in the text.

After Reading Activities

In the book, different colors of skateboards and their parts are mentioned. Have any of the children used a skateboard before? What color was it? Where did they ride it to? Ask the children to draw and color a picture of a skateboard. What color are its wheels? What color is the deck? Ask them to draw an environment or place around the skateboard. Where would they like to ride their skateboards? Have the readers share their pictures with the group and discuss their answers.

Tadpole Books are published by Jump!, 5357 Penn Avenue South, Minneapolis, MN 55419, www.jumplibrary.com

Copyright ©2019 Jump. International copyright reserved in all countries. No part of this book may be reproduced in any form without written permission from the publisher.

Editor: Jenna Trnka **Designer:** Anna Peterson

Photo Credits: Zoonar GmbH/Alamy, cover; LightFieldStudios/iStock, 1; FamVeld/Shutterstock, 2–3, 16bm; al7/Shutterstock, 4–5, 10–11 (foreground), 16fl, 16tm; Mark Nazh/Shutterstock, 6–7, 16br; ABO PHOTOGRAPHY/Shutterstock, 8–9, 16tr; sathaporn/Shutterstock, 10–11 (background); Blue Jean Images/Getty, 12–13, 16bl; kate_sept2004/iStock, 14–15.

Library of Congress Cataloging-in-Publication Data
Names: Kenan, Tessa, author.
Title: Skateboards / by Tessa Kenan.
Description: Minneapolis, MN : Jump!, Inc., (2018) | Series: Let's go! | Includes index.
Identifiers: LCCN 2017061698 (print) | LCCN 2018002436 (ebook) | ISBN 9781624969966 (ebook) | ISBN 9781624969942 (hardcover : alk. paper) | ISBN 9781624969959 (pbk.)
Subjects: LCSH: Skateboarding—Juvenile literature. | Skateboards—Juvenile literature. | CYAC: Skateboarding. | Skateboards. | LCGFT: Picture books. | Illustrated works.
Classification: LCC GV859.8 (ebook) | LCC GV859.8 .K445 2018 (print) | DDC 796.22—dc23
LC record available at https://lccn.loc.gov/2017061698

SKATEBOARDS

tadpole
books

LET'S GO!

SKATEBOARDS

by Tessa Kenan

TABLE OF CONTENTS

SKATEBOARDS

Skateboards help us go!

deck

See the deck.

wheel

See the wheels.

green

This one is green.

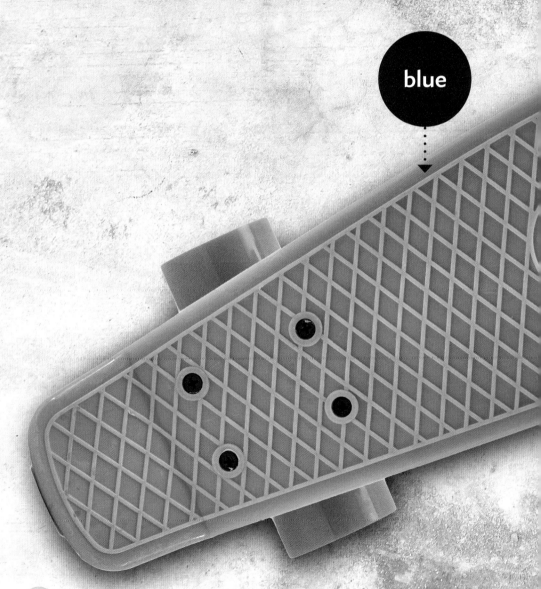

blue

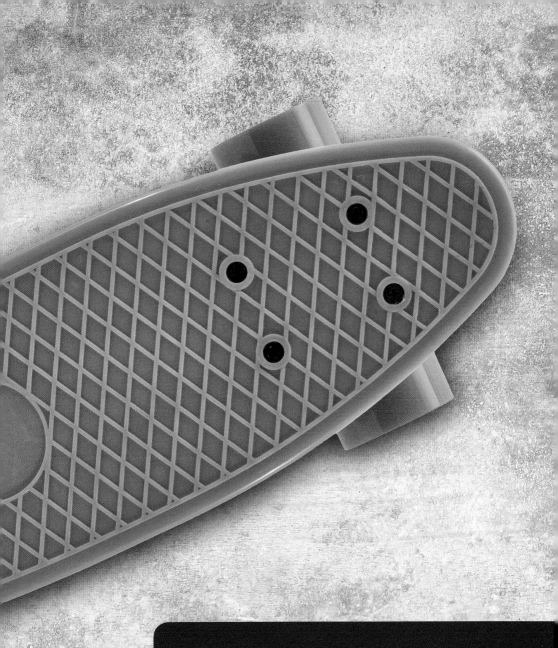

This one is blue.

red

This one is red.

Let's go!

WORDS TO KNOW

blue

deck

green

red

skateboards

wheels

INDEX